Mom, Where Does Our Milk Come From?

Children on the Homestead Series: Book 1

For my children, Rosannah, Brynlee, Ainsley, Dash, Jacob, Wynona, and Baby Nate: May you always remember your time on the homestead and our "farm school" sessions with fondness. I love the excitement each of you bring to this adventure.

To my husband David: Thank you for believing in me when I don't believe in myself and for pushing me to achieve my dreams. This book (and future books) wouldn't be possible without you sharing the load! I love you!

Mom, Where Does Our Milk Come From?

Children on the Homestead Series: Book 1

By Brittany Kanagy

Illustrated By Britton Hogg

One hot summer day, in late afternoon, Wynona and her friend, Zoey, went inside Wynona's house to take a break from the heat. In the kitchen, they found Wynona's mom and sister, Ainsley, gathering ingredients to make a batch of homemade ice cream.

 "What flavor?" Wynona asked.

Ainsley held up a bowl of freshly diced peaches. "Peach. Your favorite," she said.

1

While Ainsley added the ice cream mix to their large electric ice cream maker, Wynona decided to pour herself and Zoey an ice-cold glass of milk.

Zoey watched Wynona pouring from the large serving jars. "This milk looks different from ours at home." Zoey stated. "Mrs. Kanagy, where does your milk come from?"

"Great question!" Mom said with a twinkle in her eye.

Wynona knew that look. Mom loved teaching about life on the homestead, especially where their food came from. They were about to have another, "farm school lesson."

"Most families buy their milk from the grocery store in ready-to-go disposable containers," Mom began.

"That's what my mom does," said Zoey.

"The milk comes from dairies all over the country. The cows are milked, and the milk is then sent in big trucks to a processing facility where it gets pasteurized and homogenized."

"Pasture-what?" asked Zoey.

"Pasteurization is a process where the milk is heated to kill off any germs that may have found their way into the milk during transportation to the bottling facility."

"Oh, that's a good idea; germs can make you sick," said Wynona.

"That's right; they can," Mom responded, "but did you know that milk also has good germs, or bacteria, that make your tummy, healthy and strong?"

"There are good bacteria?" exclaimed Wynona.

"There sure are, but when milk is pasteurized, it kills the good bacteria right along with the bad. We lose some of the parts that make milk so good for us."

"Wow!' said Zoey. "What about that other word? Homogenize. What does that mean?"

"Homogenization is a process that breaks up the cream into very small particles which helps them stay mixed into the milk. This is done by pushing the milk through a series of small openings or screens at very high pressures. If the milk is not homogenized, the cream will separate and rise to the top of the jar."

"That's what our milk does." Wynona said, pointing to the large serving jar on the table. "We have to shake our milk before we use it, that means it's not homogenized."

"That's right," Mom smiled. "While these processes have their benefits, they aren't always needed. When cows are kept clean and healthy, and their milk is handled correctly, we don't need to pasteurize or homogenize it. This allows the milk to keep the good bacteria and extra vitamins that help our bodies grow strong. When milk is not pasteurized or homogenized, like ours, it is called 'raw milk.'"

By now the ice cream machine had been filled and was humming happily as it chilled and mixed the milky ingredients.

"We don't buy our milk from the store," Wynona told Zoey. "We get ours from right here on the farm."

"Zoey, would you like to see how we get our milk?" asked Mom.

Zoey nodded her head.

"Ainsley, can you keep an eye on the ice cream while Zoey, Wynona, and I visit Eleanor?" Mom asked.

"Sure," Ainsley responded, "I have some fresh cream that has been sitting out all morning, waiting to be made into butter. I can do that while I'm here in the kitchen."

"That's a great idea," Mom said as she slipped on her barn boots. Wynona and Zoey finished their milk and placed the empty glasses in the sink.

On their way to the barn, Wynona asked, "Are we going to milk Eleanor right now?"

Mom laughed, "It just so happens that it's time for her evening milking." She looked at Zoey, "We milk Eleanor in the early morning and again in the evening; about every twelve hours. Sometimes her schedule is different. For example, when her baby, Merida, was young, we did what's called "calf sharing" meaning we only milked her once a day, and the rest of the time Merida was able to drink the milk. Just like you, when you were a baby, young cows need their mother's milk to grow big and strong. But now that Merida is older, she eats hay and grain, so we get to keep more of Eleanor's milk. Cows must give birth to produce milk, and dairy cows produce a lot of milk, which makes them perfectly designed to share with us."

As they entered the area of the barn, which Mom called the milking parlor, Zoey saw the big wooden stanchion and asked, "Is that where Eleanor stands to be milked?"

"It is!" Mom exclaimed. "She comes in through this gate, and her head fits perfectly between these two boards. Once her head is in, I push the boards together so she stays in this spot the whole time I'm milking her."

"Doesn't it scare her?" Wynona asked, poking her own head through the opening.

"Not at all," Mom said cheerily. "In fact, she enjoys it because she knows she gets a special treat. While I am milking her, she gets a scoop of grain and alfalfa pellets, which is like your getting a scoop of ice cream."

"So, it's like she gets a snack while being milked." Wynona said.

"Yes," Mom agreed, "and she loves her snacks!" Mom poured a scoop of grain and alfalfa pellets into the feed trough. Like clockwork, Eleanor the cow was standing at the gate.

"Wow! You didn't even have to call her!" Zoey said amazed.

"No," Mom said amused, "dairy cows love their routine. Usually, she is already standing here waiting on me! Come with me into the next room to get our milking machine ready."

The next room was different than the milking parlor. There was a large double sink, shelves holding clean jars and other supplies, and even a dishwasher.

"Some people who milk a family cow don't have a separate processing room like we have; they process and wash everything in their kitchen," Mom began. "Some families don't use a milking machine either. When we first began milking, we milked with our hands, squirting the milk into a simple metal bucket. Many families use this method every day. On our farm, this is the room where we process the milk and store our milking equipment to keep it out of the dusty barn," Mom said, as she pointed to the milking machine over in the corner. It was on a special cart with wheels.

Mom explained first that they must sterilize the machine to make sure it's nice and clean. She filled up the sink with hot water and a special dairy soap and sucked it up with what she called, "the claw."

Wynona giggled to her friend, "That part of the machine reminds me of a long-legged bug!"

Once that was finished, Mom dumped the water out of the large metal bucket attached to the machine and said they were ready to milk.

They wheeled the milking machine into the milking parlor. Mom opened the gate and Eleanor came right in and went directly to her spot in the stanchion!

Just as she explained, Mom closed the boards by Eleanor's head, and Eleanor continued munching on her treat. Mom took her place beside the cow and, with a clean rag, began wiping off Eleanor's udder.

"When a cow lies down in the field, dirt can get on the udder and into the teats," Mom began. "We want to make sure we clean her off very well before we attach the machine." When the udders were clean on the outside, Mom squirted milk from each teat into a separate cup to make sure all the dirt had been washed away.

"We don't want any dirt or hay in our milk," Mom chuckled.

Next, Mom flipped the claw upside down and attached the "legs" to each of Eleanor's four teats. Immediately, the milk began to flow through the tubes and into the attached bucket. After the machine was finished milking, Mom unhooked the claw and sprayed Eleanor's udder with a special disinfectant spray.

Mom explained, "This spray helps to keep the cow's udder healthy which in turn keeps the milk healthy." They then wheeled the machine back into the processing room.

"What do we do now? Zoey asked.

"Well," Mom began, "next we have to strain the milk just in case any dirt or trash did find its way into the milk."

Mom set up a few clean serving jars and a large funnel. Inside the funnel she placed a round paper-like disk. She explained this was to catch anything that might have fallen into the milk. Mom then opened the top of the milking bucket.

Zoey peered in. "Look at all that milk!" she exclaimed.

Mom picked up the full bucket and began slowly pouring the milk into the funnel that was perched on the prepared jars. As the milk ran through the filter, the jar began to fill. When that jar was full, Mom moved the filter to another jar and continued pouring. Very soon they had two, full gallon jars of milk on the counter.

"Now they are ready to chill!" Mom said satisfied.

"Chill?" Zoey asked.

"Yes," Mom began, "remember those bacteria we discussed earlier? If we cool down the milk quickly, it reduces the number of bad bacteria and keeps them from growing. It also helps to keep the milk fresh longer."

After labeling the jars with the date, she placed them in a cooler filled with ice water.

"The jars sit in the ice water to cool down. We want the temperature to go down to 35-40° Fahrenheit within one hour of milking. This keeps the milk yummy to drink," Mom said. "Then we transfer them to the refrigerator."

After they cleaned the milking machine with another round of special dairy soap and hot water, Eleanor was finished with her snack. She was ready to go back into the pasture. Mom pushed the boards away and Eleanor backed out the gate, just as seamlessly as she had come in. Wynona and Zoey helped tidy up the stanchion, and they headed back inside.

Mom and the girls found Ainsley in the kitchen right where they had left her, only now she had two pounds of fresh butter ready for the refrigerator.

"Perfect timing!" Ainsley exclaimed as the girls joined her at the kitchen counter.

"You can both help me finish this last batch of butter before the ice cream is ready."

"I've never made butter before," Zoey said timidly.

"It's easy!" Wynona said reassuringly. "We will show you!"

Mom left the girls making butter while she ventured back outside to help Dad finish the evening chores.

Ainsley handed Zoey a lidded jar, half-filled with cream.

"Shake this," Ainsley said. Zoey started shaking the jar. Shaking, shaking, shaking some more. After a few minutes of shaking, she noticed that the cream had started to change. It was getting thicker, and the sloshing sound in the jar was getting quieter.

"What's happening?" Zoey asked.

"Keep shaking; you're almost there!" Wynona said.

Just when her arms were starting to get tired from all of the shaking, Zoey felt a, "thump, thumping," in the jar. Inside, she saw a light yellow lump sitting in a cloudy liquid.

"Is that butter?" Zoey asked her friend.

"Yes! Great job! You did it!" Wynona cheered.

"Now it's time to rinse the butter!" Ainsley said as she took the jar and drained the liquid off. She then dumped the butter in a bowl with very cold water and used a spoon to mash and roll the butter over and over until the water was cloudy. She then poured off the cloudy water and added fresh water to the bowl. Ainsley explained that this was to remove all the buttermilk which was the cloudy liquid in the jar.

"Removing as much buttermilk as you can helps the butter to stay fresh longer," she said.

Ainsley repeated this process once more and this time, the water stayed clear. After draining it a final time, Ainsley mixed in a little sprinkle of salt for extra flavor and put the butter into molds which shaped the butter into sticks, like the sticks that you find in the store.

"Not everyone uses molds like we do," Ainsley explained. "Some people store their butter in jars or wrap it in plastic wrap."

With that, Ainsley took a portion of the butter, rolled it into a ball, and wrapped it tightly with plastic wrap. "You can take this batch home with you Zoey."

Ainsley placed the wrapped ball and butter filled molds in the refrigerator to chill. "Once cold, we will pop the sticks out and store in it a container in the refrigerator or freezer until we need it," she said.

It was just then that the ice cream maker started to slow its mixing. Ainsley checked the contents and sure enough, the ice cream was ready.

"Go gather everyone from outside," Ainsley said excitedly, "It's time for ice cream!"

When the family came inside, bowls of fresh, peach ice cream were waiting for them on the table. As everyone enjoyed their ice cream, Wynona and Zoey told them about their visit to the barn and what Mom taught them about raw milk.

"Now I know where raw milk comes from!" Zoey beamed.

Ainsley told them about the fresh butter that she and the girls had made.

"I'm excited to share some with my family!" Zoey said.

Everyone listened as they ate their treat happily. What a great day on the farm!

Ainsley and Wynona's Homemade Butter

Ingredients:

- Heavy Cream
- Salt (Optional)
- Cold Water (You can use ice to lower the temperature of the water.)
- Quart Jar or Similar Container with Sealable Lid
- Mixing bowl
- Spoon (for mixing and mashing the butter)
- Plastic Wrap (or Butter Mold)

Directions:

- Let heavy cream sit out of refrigerator until it is room temperature or at least one hour.
- Pour heavy cream in quart jar until it reaches just under the halfway mark. (DO NOT overfill jar, the cream needs room to agitate to become butter.) Seal lid and shake.
- Continue shaking until the cream breaks and a clump of butter forms. You can pass the jar to different family members if the little one's arms tire quickly. This process can take 15-20 minutes, depending on the temperature of the cream.
- When the butter forms, drain off the excess liquid (uncultured buttermilk) and place the solid butter in the bowl of cold water. Use spoon to begin kneading the butter to get excess buttermilk out.
- When water becomes cloudy, change out for fresh cold water.
- Make sure water stays cold or the butter will become too soft.
- After a few washes you can knead the butter by hand in the bowl of cold water to squeeze out the remaining pockets of buttermilk.
- When the water remains clean after washing, you can remove the butter from the water and squeeze excess water from the ball.
- Discard the water from bowl and replace butter.
- Knead in salt to taste.
- If using molds, you can now press the butter into the molds and chill until hard.
- If using plastic wrap: Lay a square of plastic wrap on the
- counter. Place butter in the center and fold plastic wrap around it.
- You can shape the butter into a ball or slightly roll it into a "log" shape for slicing.
- Use butter immediately or store it in the refrigerator.

ABOUT THE AUTHOR

Hi, I'm Brittany, a homeschooling, homesteading mother of 6, with number 7 on the way (at the time of this publishing). I live with my family in rural South Carolina and, when I find the time, I enjoy crafting, sewing, crochet, and spoiling our growing herd of Jersey cattle. Our farm has pigs, cows, chickens, dogs, and a large garden to keep us busy. I am a night-owl and TV show binge-watcher who tends to hyper-fixate on too many projects at once. You can also find homestead related videos and follow our family farm experiences on YouTube and across social media at Boundary Creek Farm.

ABOUT THE ILLUSTRATOR

Hi, I'm Britton, but you can call me Bee! I live in South Carolina with my parents and my old dog, Lynard. I've been drawing most of my life and have enjoyed branching out into illustrating books. Just to keep things interesting, I also have a degree in Esthetics, but art has always been my focus. When I'm not working on art commissions or other projects, I like to post on TikTok and hang out with my friends. I'm very in-tune with my inner-child and love watching cartoons like Owl House and My Little Pony. My best work is done after midnight and with a glass of chocolate milk next to me. You can also find me on TikTok and Instagram: @BDArts.

www.ingramcontent.com/pod-product-compliance
Lightning Source LLC
LaVergne TN
LVHW010032070426
835508LV00005B/304